THE URBAN WOODSMAN

Photography: Dean Hearne
Design: Tina Smith

K

Kyle Books
www.kylebooks.co.uk

THE URBAN
WOODSMAN

A MODERN GUIDE TO CARVING SPOONS, BOWLS & BOARDS

MAX BAINBRIDGE

To my Nana, Jean Gray

First published in Great Britain in 2016
by Kyle Cathie Ltd
Part of Octopus Publishing Group Limited
Carmelite House, 50 Victoria Embankment
London, EC4Y 0DZ
www.kylebooks.co.uk

10 9 8 7

ISBN 978 0 85783 377 8

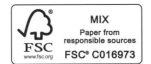

Text © 2016 Max Bainbridge
Design © 2016 Kyle Books
Photography © 2016 Dean Hearne

Designer: Tina Smith
Photographer: Dean Hearne
Stylist: Jeska Hearne
Project Editor: Sophie Allen
Copy Editor: Barbara Bonsor
Editorial Assistant: Hannah Coughlin
Production: Nic Jones, Gemma John and Lisa Pinnell

A Cataloguing in Publication record for this title is available from the British Library.

Printed and bound in China

CONTENTS

INTRODUCTION

Wood has fascinated me for as long as I can remember. Everything from its smell and texture, to its grain and colour has always intrigued me, and I have always known it would be something I would work with. It is such a versatile and beautiful material that can be used in endless different applications. One of my earliest childhood memories is firing a bow and arrow that I had made in our back garden. It had carved notches where the string sat at each end, and a handle carved into the bark revealing bright, white sapwood. I think it was this revelation that had such a lasting effect on me: the moment that I understood you could take a tree branch, and by the simple act of cutting, transform it into something useful – something that had a function. With a simple intervention you can reveal qualities in the wood that at first glance are not visible. It is this infinite potential that

'Being a maker is not just a job, it is a way of life'

leaves me feeling just as amazed and excited today as it did when I made that first cut all those years ago. I have been a 'maker' all my life and it is only in the past three years that I have started to work with wood as a craft. I made a conscious decision to hone my need to work with my hands into a set of skills. Being able to then apply these skills to create objects that are not only beautiful in their form, but also functional and a pleasure to use, has become the driving force behind my work. Being a maker, woodworker, craftsman, carver, artist (whatever you want to call it), is not just a job, it is a way of life. Whenever I give an interview or talk to someone about what I do, I find myself coming back to the same way of phrasing it, and that is to say that 'I live what I do'. It is all-consuming. I am never not at work and I never have a day off. I think this is true of anyone who makes things or has a craft. I don't just do this as a means to an end – I do this full stop. There is never an end point, and that is what I find so exciting. My work is a process that is constantly evolving, constantly changing, and because of that I am constantly learning. I have approached writing this book in the same way that I would start to design a new shape of spoon or work with a new species of wood. It has been both daunting and exciting in equal measure. I have had to examine every aspect of my making process, break it down into separate steps and then try to put them all back together on paper in a way that communicates my love of what I do. Writing this book has made me look at the way I use the tools I am working with and how much I actually understand the nature of wood itself. It has made me scrutinise every aspect of my own methods and has taught me as much about my own craft as I hope to impart to my readers.

I hope that by writing this book I can excite other people about the craft of carving and the magic of making. It is important for me to pass on the skills I have learned in the hope that others will get the same joy and satisfaction from the making process as I do. It is fundamental that people

'Everything is designed to have a use, and everything that gets made is useful'

realise that working wood is something that everyone can do; you just need to have a starting point and a determination to learn. I started with a book, some YouTube videos and a large box of plasters. Three years later I am running my full-time business Forest + Found with my partner Abigail, making functional objects using traditional skills with contemporary design. In this book I will explore different techniques and processes including carving, filing, scorching, sanding and waxing, all of which will be used to make objects that can be used in your home every day. If something doesn't have an actual function then it doesn't usually leave the workshop. 'Everything is designed to have a use, and everything that gets made is useful.'

Living in the city has an effect on everything I make: it determines where I work, the materials I use, and it influences aspects of my design process. Being based in Walthamstow in East London, I am surrounded by the

most diverse sources of both inspiration and materials. It is so important when living and working in a city to seek out the green spaces. It is these places that give you a change of environment and allow you time to breathe and think. I am fortunate to be in close proximity to Epping Forest, which covers 2,400 hectares of ancient woodland between the borders of North-East London and Essex. It is somewhere that I visit regularly, not only to stock up on a good selection of native hardwoods, but also to escape the hustle and bustle of London life.

Being in an urban environment has meant I have had to seek out different sources of wood that can provide a sustainable and regular supply of material to work with. This does not mean just seeking out forests and green spaces. As well as working with forestry staff, I have also built up relationships with furniture- and cabinetmakers over the years. Getting to know other craftspeople can result in a regular supply of hardwood that would otherwise be burnt or go to landfill. Being able to take a by-product

'You can get hold of workable timber from just about anywhere'

of someone else's industry and transform it into something useful is a very important part of how I work. I think it is vital to understand that you can get hold of workable timber from just about anywhere. As long as you go through the proper channels and take the time to talk to people, most of the time they will be more than willing to help. Whether you live in a large city or a small village, all the information I have compiled in this book is just as valid and useful. It will enable you to discover what is available to use and where to go to find it.

One of the most important things to me is that I enjoy what I do. Sometimes carving can be really hard work. You might get to a stage in a project that proves particularly difficult or stubborn and it is then that I like to take five minutes to have a breather and more often than not make a cup of tea. It is far more productive to step back and think of a solution rather than continue and get frustrated. I have learned the hard way that by ploughing on you can end up making silly mistakes or worse, giving yourself an injury. Health and safety is something I take very seriously and with a few simple checks and precautions it is something that doesn't need to get in the way or take up much time. The main things to think about are yourself, your surroundings, your materials and your tools. Give yourself time before starting a new project to take note of what you are going to make, what tools and materials you will need, where you are going to be working and most importantly that you feel up to the challenge. Trying to work if you are stressed, tired or your mind is not focused can be dangerous to yourself as well as others around you. The projects in this book are designed to build on your skill levels at each stage, so you should feel confident and excited about taking on each new challenge. Carving is at its most enjoyable when you are not constrained by a deadline. I want to encourage people to understand that craft takes time and is always the better for it.

'Understand that craft takes time and is always the better for it'

My practice has always been involved in contemporary design, but underpinning this is the constant narrative of traditional craft. I hope that people can use this book as a springboard to learning a new way of working that allows them to go on to design and make their own things. I want to emphasise that as well as making spoons, woodcarving can benefit you in a lot of ways. It can improve your state of mind by letting you step out of modern fast-paced living and slowing things down. As you concentrate on achieving the perfect cut on the edge of a board or sweep of a handle, you begin to understand the subtleties that wood affords. Wherever you are in the world, carving allows the simple pleasure of being in touch with the outdoors and learning how to make use of our natural resources. I hope that by the end of this book you will have the knowledge and excitement to carry on exploring this craft that I have fallen in love with.

SOURCING WOOD

Knowing where to get your materials from can make all the difference when starting to learn how to carve. Finding a reliable source of timber at a relatively low cost will allow you to experiment and play without worrying about how much your materials have cost you. There are four main sources I get my wood from, all of which do not cost very much and sometimes can even be free.

The Local Forestry Commission

I am fortunate enough to be a short car drive away from Epping Forest, which is run by the City of London Corporation. I did a bit of research and was able to get in contact with one of the men from the Forestry Commission. He was more than happy to show me what species of trees they manage and let me hunt through the huge piles of wood they amass as part of the regular management of the forest.

I work a lot with silver birch as it is a fast growing species and is constantly being thinned out to maintain a healthy balance within the forest. Although silver birch is the most common wood available at Epping, there are also quite a few different varieties of British hardwoods there. Exactly what wood is available depends on whether a tree needs storm-damaged limbs removing or if one gets rot and needs to be taken down safely. However, I find that sourcing wood this way is a great way to work as you are constantly surprised and challenged by what is available. It makes you flexible with your designs and shapes, as you cannot rely on getting a specific type of wood time and time again. It is this variety that I find so exciting and you will find the same diversity and availability of species working with any local

Forestry Commission that you come across.

Having made contact with the Forestry Commission at Epping, I now arrange to meet one of the forestry workers at their base, and we go out to a site within the forest where they have been working so I can see what is available. They are happy for me to sift through and pick and choose until I have a car full of wood. The arrangement I have is to make a small donation to the Forestry Commission as a token of appreciation and spread the word about the great work they are doing. You will find every Commission will want to work differently, but if you take the time to explain who you are and what it is you want the wood for, people are usually more than willing to help. It is all about going through the right channels and being respectful of people and their time. I am more than happy to work around the schedules of the people who work in Epping as it means I can get a fantastic source of sustainable, native hardwoods. It also means I get to spend a morning in a beautiful green space and build up working relationships with local authorities.

Tree Surgeons

The ability to tune in to the sound of a chainsaw nearby can be a very worthwhile skill. On several occasions I have dropped whatever I was doing at the time and dashed out to track down the sound of a chainsaw. Tree surgeons operate all over, from small towns to big cities. If you see tree surgeons at work, it is always worth asking them what they are working on and if they would be willing to let you take a few bits of what they are cutting down. It is important to always make sure you wait until it is safe to approach them, for their and your own safety. When the saw stops and you can see them moving wood to their truck, it is usually a good time to go and speak to them.

Tree surgeons can be a fantastic source of native hardwoods as well as a way of getting hold of some more varied and exotic varieties of wood. A lot of the time the smaller branches go straight through the chipper first, so if you can stop them shredding everything in one go you can usually get yourself some good-sized pieces that are still workable.

Other Makers

Building up relationships with other makers and craftsmen can be a fantastic source of material. Not only is it important to be part of a creative community but I have also found that other people's waste materials can sometimes be perfect for what you need. I work with several joiners and cabinetmakers who produce large amounts of offcuts that they have no use for. More often than not they have to pay to get rid of excess wood, so it helps them if you are able to take this unwanted material off their hands. If you take the time to talk to people and explain what it is you do and what you are looking for, then through these conversations, mutual working relationships are born.

Timber Merchants

Some timber merchants, usually the ones specialising in hardwoods, will keep a good selection of offcuts. One close to me has an onsite sawmill where they can cut, plane and rip wood to size for their customers, which inevitably produces offcuts in varying shapes and sizes, some of which can be just the right size and thickness for what I am looking for.

It is always worth going to have a rummage around a timber yard if they have a place where they keep their offcuts, as you can stumble across some really interesting species of wood and, because of the small sizes, they are usually willing to let you have them for a very reasonable price. Bare in mind that not every timber merchant specialises in native British hardwoods, so it is worth doing some research and finding one that you like.

CHOOSING WOOD

Choosing the correct type of wood for your project is crucial. Getting to know the difference between hardwoods and softwoods will allow you to pick the right species and type of wood to work with. Throughout this book I will be using a variety of different hardwoods. Softwoods are not really suitable for carving. They have a widely spaced grain and their soft surface makes them prone to tearing. Softwood can also be quite porous so is not suitable for making utensils and bowls that will come into contact with food or liquid. Hardwoods, on the other hand, tend to be close-grained and very strong, ideal for making objects that are used daily.

In my day-to-day practice, I work with a selection of green hardwood, reclaimed hardwood and hardwood offcuts. The term 'green wood' refers to wood that has been freshly cut and still holds a lot of moisture, making it much easier to work with than seasoned wood, which has been left to dry over time. Both green wood and seasoned wood each have their advantages and disadvantages when carving. Green wood is far easier to work with as the high moisture content makes the fibres of the wood softer and more flexible. This allows the blade of your knife to cut through the fibres with greater ease. However, unlike seasoned wood, it can crack and warp as it dries. Seasoned wood is much tougher to carve, as the fibres, being dry, are very hard and rigid. You will find your knives need to be sharpened more frequently when working seasoned wood, but you will be able to rely on its stability

'Getting to know the difference between hardwoods and softwoods will allow you to pick the right species'

species it is. It is always worth doing some research online to firstly identify the species, which is best done by looking at the bark and shape of leaves, and secondly to make sure that what you have gathered and found is not poisonous. If you are getting it from a timber merchant, Forestry Commission or tree surgeon then make sure to ask them what kind of wood it is, but if you are not sure there are some great websites you can use to check: www.wood-database.com is my go-to site to identify a species

---

'Adapt designs and work with the character of the material'

---

as all cracks and warps have already happened during the drying process. I wanted to use both green and seasoned wood in this book to show that if you know how to approach working with them, and understand that a green piece of birch will behave differently to a seasoned piece of birch, it is well worth working with both. It offers you twice as much scope for getting your hands on usable timber and gives you an insight into which kinds of wood are best suited for the project you have in your head. You will find that if you are sourcing wood from tree surgeons or Forestry Commissions, it will most likely be green and freshly cut. If you have managed to get hold of hardwood offcuts or scraps from a timber merchant, the likelihood is that these have been kiln-dried and well seasoned. You can season green wood yourself, which means storing it in a well ventilated dry space, such as a garden shed, and leaving it for prolonged periods of time. This can sometimes take up to two years for wood to completely dry out.

You also have to think about what kind of wood you are sourcing, especially if you are not sure what

and check for toxicity. It takes a few minutes of research to give you peace of mind that you can use your wood safely.

Storing wood is also something you need to think about. Seasoned hardwood and offcuts can be stored easily enough without having to really do anything. They just need to be in dry conditions and not in direct contact with a heat source. Green wood, however, requires a little bit more attention. If you are going to be working with it straight away then you don't need to worry about storing it, but if you want to be able to store wood to work over time then you need to take a few simple steps. There are lots of different ways people store green

cracks if they appear. Some of my favourite objects I have made have been the result of using timber that has developed cracks as I have been working with it. It teaches you how to adapt designs and work with the character of the material.

I have tried to use a different species of hardwood for each project in the book to demonstrate the wide variety of timber that is readily available. You can, of course, make all of the projects in this book from one type of wood. I have used green oak for the small bowl for example, but there is no reason

wood. The main goals are to prevent it from drying out too quickly and splitting. You can buy all sorts of wax sealants and compounds, which work well but can be quite expensive. I have seen people put green wood in the freezer and even in large barrels of water covered in candle wax. I think it is worth experimenting to see what works best for you, but I always recommend simplicity. I tend to use PVA glue on the end of thinner branches and lengths of green wood to seal the moisture in. If I am cutting up some larger logs then I tend to split them in half, and wrap them in clingfilm or plastic bin bags, and keep them in a cool dark place. It is important to split any logs in half as, if left whole, any evaporating moisture will cause the wood to shrink, which builds up tension and results in cracks and splits opening up. If left, the cracks can travel the full length of the log inside, making your life difficult when trying to find a solid piece to work with. There is, however, only so much you can do. Wood is a natural material and there is always going to be a level of unpredictability to it. Sometimes you just have to go with it and work with the splits and

'Wood is a natural material and there is always going to be a level of unpredictability to it'

you couldn't use silver birch or sweet chestnut instead. I think it is always nice to work with what is available locally to you and, especially if you are just starting out, it is great to be able to source wood close by. In each project I give a brief explanation of why I have chosen to work with each different wood. You can choose to follow by my example, but in no way is it a rule to stick by. I always choose wood for its practicality, but often when there are several suitable kinds of wood, I then make a choice based on aesthetics and how I want an object to look.

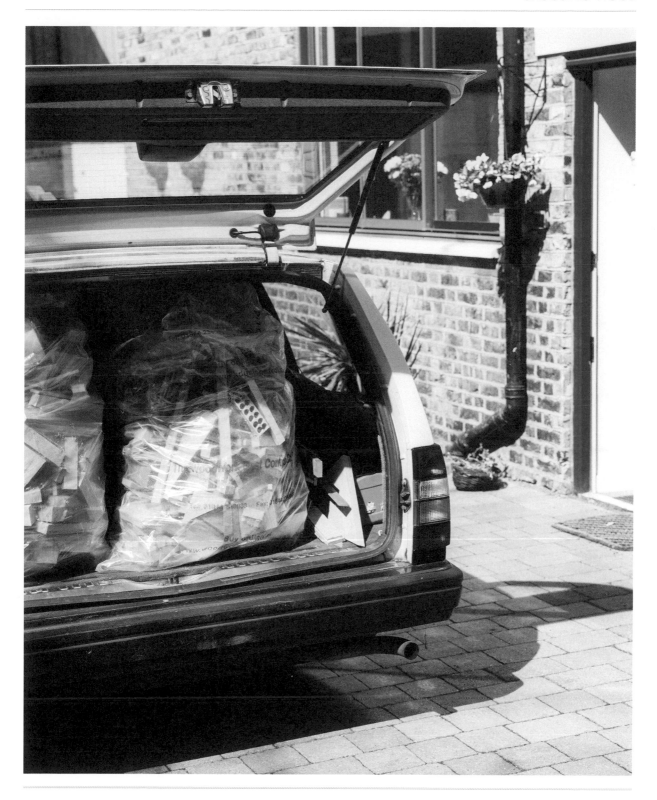

WOOD TYPES

1. Oak (Green)
When green, oak can be easily worked with hand tools, making it a very suitable choice for bowls and vessels.

2. Silver Birch
Silver birch can be used for a wide range of items. Its uniform grain and texture make it a very reliable carving material. It has the ability to be both strong and lightweight at the same time.

3. Reclaimed Oak
Oak is incredibly strong and robust. It's perfect for items that will see a lot of day to day use. When seasoned, it can be quite tough to work with but the finished item will last.

4. Sweet Chestnut
Sweet chestnut is both strong and flexible. It has a beautiful grain and texture so is ideal for items that will be used on a daily basis.

5

6   **7**

8

5. Reclaimed Maple
Its close uniform grain makes maple the perfect choice of wood to prepare, serve and cut food on. It's incredibly hard-wearing and stands up well to daily use.

6. Reclaimed Cherry
Cherry is an exceptionally strong hardwood. Its close grain makes it ideal for coming into contact with moisture.

7. Cherry (Green)
Cherry is great to work with when it's green and then hardens as it dries out, which means you can carve the handle of a spoon longer and thinner whilst still maintaining strength.

8. Reclaimed American Black Walnut
Walnut is a fantastically versatile hardwood. It's perfect for making cooking utensils due to its strength and durability.

TOOLS

Having the right tools for the job is essential. The tools I use in this book are relatively inexpensive and easy to get hold of. You don't need a huge arsenal of tools and equipment to be able to carve and make. The two main tools I use throughout this book are the crook knife and the straight knife. There are a lot of variations on the ones I will be using, but these two are tried and tested. Not only do they perform brilliantly, but they are also inexpensive and you can get hold of them from just about anywhere. For further information on sources, see page 138.

The crook knife with its distinctive curved blade is designed for hollowing or scooping out a concave form, which is why it is so perfectly suited for carving the bowls of spoons. The straight knife performs many different tasks from removing bulk waste to the fine detail of finishing cuts. You will find both of these knives in any woodcarver's tool roll and it is a great place to start when setting out. They will quickly become your essential tools from which you can build up a collection of more varied and specialised tools, if you wish to do so.

Tools in their own right are exceptionally pleasing objects. In Scandinavia there is a strong tradition of decorating carving tools, with ornately carved handles, patterned leather sheaths and painstakingly sculpted guards made from horn and antler. The same level of care and respect that goes into looking after and making the tools reflects the care that then goes into using them. It is this lesson that I try to remember when using my tools, as the best craftsmanship begins with understanding how your tools behave and work. I often find if I

am in the workshop talking to someone, I will look down and find myself carving a spoon I have picked up absentmindedly. Using my tools has become second nature to me. You start to get a feel for them, and as you do you begin to understand their weight and the way they fit in your hand. When you are comfortable with the tools you are using they almost become an extension of your hands, allowing you to work confidently.

▬▬▬

'*Tools in their own right are exceptionally pleasing objects*'

▬▬▬

As you begin to take on new challenges and projects, you will naturally find which tools are best suited for a specific job. You may find yourself working with every tool you have to create that one perfect spoon, or you may prefer to stick with one or two knives. There is no right and wrong way of reaching that end goal. Whatever works for you the best will allow you to produce the best work. This book is about encouraging you to have a go and to explore carving in a way that suits you. Each of us will find our hands like to work in different ways.

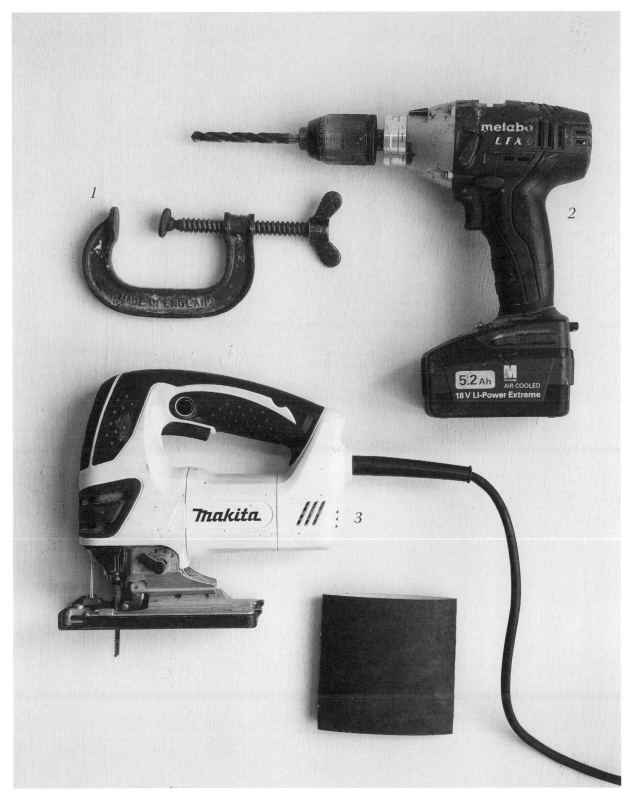

1. G Clamp

The G clamp is a really useful piece of equipment if you are working with chisels or using the reverse scoop cut with the crook knife. It allows you to secure the workpiece to a desk or workbench freeing up both hands to grip and control your tools.

2. Drill

Being able to make clean holes quickly and efficiently using a drill can make a big difference to a project. You do not need anything expensive or state of the art; as long as it works and you can use it safely then it is fit for purpose.

3. Jigsaw

I use a jigsaw for a lot of the projects in this book. It gives you the opportunity to make controlled cuts and minimise wastage as well as speeding up the process. As with the drill, you don't need to spend vast amounts of money on something that is laser guided and has lots of different features. As long as it has the power to cut through hardwood, which most jigsaws will with the correct blade, it will be fine.

4. Carving gouges

These gouges are a great addition to your tool roll. They offer you a different way of carving, and come in all different shapes and sizes. The two I will be using are relatively small and good for finer, more detailed work.

4

5

6

5. Mora 120 straight knife

This is a classic woodcarving knife, and you will find yourself using it the most throughout this book. With over a century of skill and passion behind the Mora brand, these Swedish knives have always been a go-to tool for craftsmen. The craftsmanship that goes into making each knife is tried and tested and is evident as soon as you start using one.

6. Mora 162 crook knife

This curved, double-edged blade allows you to make a variety of different rounded cuts. Using different sections of the blade you can achieve delicate refinement as well as deep, hollowing cuts. It is an extremely versatile tool.

7. Japanese saw rasp

This is quite a specialist tool but still very affordable. It allows you to shape and sculpt the surfaces of wood and remove waste material quickly and efficiently. It has a coarse and a fine side that means you can really refine the shapes you are creating.

8. Axe

The axe is a fantastically versatile tool, especially if you are working with greenwood. If I am not in my workshop, I can take an axe and two carving knives out allowing me to work just about anywhere. The axe pictured is a hatchet which, due to its small size, makes it perfect for processing smaller pieces of wood into spoon blanks.

KNIFE GRIPS

Knife grips are one of the most important elements of technique that I cover in this book. As you work your way through the projects I encourage you to revisit this chapter as you improve your understanding of how to use your knives while working. Here is a selection of different grips and cuts that will allow you to cut and shape wood efficiently and safely. Half the battle is making sure you are aware of where your fingers are positioned in relation to the blade and not to take any unnecessary risks. It doesn't take any longer to make sure you are safe when working. My advice is to take a piece of scrap wood and practise these techniques. It is always better to master the basics on waste material before starting out on a specific project.

▼ *Straight knife: push cut*

Hold the knife in your dominant hand, and use your other hand to support the workpiece. Bring your thumb from the workpiece to the top of the handle where it meets the blade. Push away from the body, which will allow you to apply the exact amount of pressure required for the cut, whilst using your dominant hand to grip the knife and control the direction of the blade. This cut can be performed either standing or sitting. Either way you will find it most comfortable and have maximum control if you work close to your body. If you imagine you have the arms of a T-Rex it will give you an idea of the position your hands should be in relation to your chest. You will use this cut the most frequently when working so it is a good idea to familiarise yourself with it early on.

▼ Straight knife: detail cut

This cut is useful for when you are getting down to the finer details of a project and for shaping and texturing the surface. Using the knife in your dominant hand and holding the workpiece in your other, bring the thumb of the supporting hand to the back of the blade. This position will change depending on the size of the workpiece and the depth of cut required. For example, on a small piece your thumb might be near the tip of the blade giving you maximum control. Using a similar motion to the push cut, apply pressure with your thumb and guide the blade with your dominant hand.

▶ Straight knife: pull cut

Support one end of the workpiece supported in your hand, and the other on your chest (wearing an apron or protective shirt is recommended). Start the cut in front of your supporting hand. Applying even pressure and keeping the blade quite flat to the surface of the wood, draw the blade towards yourself. You are not looking for a quick, powerful motion here. You are aiming for maximum control with a clear view to where the blade is going to stop. This is a very useful technique that allows you to work longer lengths of wood whilst delivering controlled and even, straight cuts. This way of working requires you to cut towards yourself, which may seem counter-intuitive and go against everything you have ever been told when using a knife, but if done safely it is like any other carving technique. Keeping your hands and fingers behind the blade is crucial for this type of cut.

◄ *Straight knife: scissor cut*

This, as the name suggests, involves the blade and the workpiece crossing one another in a similar way to the action of a pair of scissors. Working close to your body, keeping your elbows tucked in (remember the T-Rex), hold the knife in your dominant hand and the workpiece in your other. Present the blade to the surface of the wood and using your arms to power the cut, tuck both elbows into your ribs and allow your hands to be drawn apart, thus making the cut. This is a very useful way of removing both large amounts of stock material and for finer more detailed cuts. It is also a very safe way of working, as the hand which is holding the knife can't travel past a certain point away from your body as it is restricted by the position of your arms.

▼ *Crook knife: scoop cut*

Hold the crook knife in your dominant hand with the tip of the blade facing straight up. Supporting the workpiece in your other hand, present the bevel of the blade to the surface of the wood. Using the thumb of your dominant hand as a support at the back of the workpiece, roll your hand back away from yourself while making the cut towards yourself. During this cut your thumb should act as an anchor point, making sure it stays below the edge of the workpiece out of the way of the blade.

▼ Crook knife: push cut

Hold the knife in your dominant hand and the workpiece in your other. Present the blade to the surface of the wood. Using the thumb of the hand that is gripping the workpiece, apply pressure away from yourself to make the cut. This is an effective way of getting more power into the cut, allowing you to remove stock material efficiently.

▶ Crook knife: reverse scoop cut

Hold the knife in your dominant hand with the blade facing down. Make contact with the surface of the workpiece. Use the bevel of the knife to roll through the cut away from yourself, making an upward motion with your wrist as you push through the cut. The hand holding the workpiece will act as an anchor. This cut is best done on a work surface for maximum stability.

▼ Axe: Splitting Wood

Hand positioning is really important when using your axe. Here the axe is being used to split a section of branch in half. Rather than striking down with the axe onto the wood, it is placed carefully with the blade centred on the surface and then the axe is struck with a mallet – this is a far safer and more precise way to split wood. Make sure you keep a firm grip on the bottom third of the handle, keeping your arm straight and your hand away from the head of the axe.

▼ *Axe: Cutting*

When using the axe to rough out the shape of your spoon, keep your hand and fingers holding the work piece well out of the way, tucking your thumb under your fingers away from the surface you are working on. You should be looking to grip between the middle and top section of the handle, which will give you maximum control and prevent you from making bigger swings that are less easy to control. You will find the closer to the head of the axe you grip the handle the smaller your cuts will become, this allows you to make smaller, finer cuts on the work piece.

1

EATING SPOON

Create an eating spoon from silver birch

The eating spoon is something that has been made throughout history in many different shapes and sizes. It is one of the most utilitarian of spoons I make and probably gets the most use, but it remains one of the most elegant in its simplicity and form. The shape has evolved with every one I have made, tweaking the size of the bowl or altering the length of the handle. All these adjustments have resulted in a spoon that has the right proportions and balance to make a utensil that is a joy to eat with. The aim is to create a spoon that resonates with you and becomes something that you look forward to using every day.

Tools:
axe
mallet (a section of branch will also work well)
pencil
template (paper/card)
crook knife
straight knife
sandpaper
beeswax salve
cloth

Wood:
silver birch

Selecting the right piece of wood is a really important part of the process. For this project I use silver birch. It's a fantastically versatile species of wood and a great starting point for carving. Select a section of branch that has as few knots as possible so that you have enough workable and uninterrupted wood once the log has been split.

1 Place the birch log on a stable cutting block (a large round log serves as a brilliant chopping block). Now place the axe in line with the middle of the end of the piece of timber. Using the mallet, strike down, taking care to hit the back of the axe head and not the handle.

2 Once you have two halves of log, choose the one with the flattest face. Mark out a template on thick paper or card and cut out. Draw around your template, marking out your design in the centre of the piece of wood. Start to cut away with the axe to rough out the spoon blank, removing the stock material. Always work cutting from the middle of the log down to your cutting block, making sure your axe never comes near your hands. You can keep moving and turning the blank as you shape.

3 Once you have your spoon roughed out, the next step is to carve the bowl. Using the crook knife and scoop cut, work across the grain from the far side of the bowl towards yourself. You won't need to apply a lot of pressure with the knife, as the wood is green it gives very little resistance to the blade, which makes it very easy to work.

4 Now that you have hollowed out the bowl of the spoon, you can start to shape and refine the back of the spoon with the straight knife, using the push cut. Make sure to work in one direction from the middle of the back of the spoon up, and then change direction working from the middle down to the shoulders. This should stop you cutting against the grain and experiencing unnecessary resistance.

5 After you have shaped the back of the spoon, you can work on refining the handle and the transition of the shoulders with the straight knife by using a combination of the pull cut and push cut. Once your general shape emerges, you can start using the detail cut to refine areas of your design.

6 Now that you have refined the shape and are happy with the balance and form of the spoon, you can start to sand. The one rule to remember here is always to sand with the grain, this will ensure that you achieve a silky smooth finish and avoid creating scratches by sanding across the grain, which are then difficult to get out. Work your way up through the grits, starting at 120grit moving through to 320grit, until you are happy with the surface finish.

7 Apply a generous coat of the beeswax salve with a clean cloth and allow it to soak in overnight. The following morning you can give the spoon a good rub all over to work in any remaining salve and to polish the surface.

2

SPATULA

Using cherry offcuts to create a spatula

The design for this spatula came about from an offcut of a cooking spoon. I had trimmed the back down and was about to throw the leftover scrap into the wood burner when I realised there was scope to develop the shape, and with a bit of playing around this simple but elegant spatula was formed. The beauty of this design is that it only requires a really thin piece of wood, allowing you to use even the most unremarkable pieces of offcuts. It is also a good utensil to practise honing your skills using the straight knife. If you happen to have a piece of wood that is close to the final shape, then you may not need to use a jigsaw to cut out the template, just use the straight knife to remove the waste material.

Tools:
pencil
template (paper/card)
jigsaw with curve cut blade
straight knife
sandpaper
cloth
beeswax salve

Wood:
cherry

The piece of cherry I use in this project came from a local timber merchant, which is the best place to look if you want a small, inexpensive piece of wood. Cherry is a strong hardwood, which is perfect for making utensils that have long handles and will be used for stirring. It is important to choose a wood that will stand up to its end use.

1 Use a template to mark out the shape of your spatula. It is a good idea to think carefully about the handle length as this will have an impact on how easy it is to use. You can always take wood away, but you cannot put it back, so I advise keeping the handle a little longer than required when cutting it out. You can always shorten it later.

2 Cut out the spatula blank using a jigsaw with a curve cut blade. You can purchase a curve cut blade from your local DIY store. The reason I stipulate this specific blade is that it makes cutting curved shapes far more accurate and safe.

3 Work on shaping the head of the spatula first with the straight knife. Use the scissor cut method to remove waste from the flat face of your spatula on both sides until you have a thickness you are happy with.

4 Now use the detail cut to refine the shape and carefully cut the bevel on the edge of the spatula head. This is crucial for the spatula's end function as this bevel allows you to cook and stir with ease.

5 The pull cut works well to remove long lengths of waste as you fashion the handle. With the head of the spatula held in your hand, and the handle resting on your chest, work the cuts towards your body to begin shaping the handle. To maintain smooth cuts you will need to turn the workpiece so that you are holding the end of the handle with the head against your chest. This change of direction in cuts stops you from cutting through the grain and gives you a smooth, even finish.

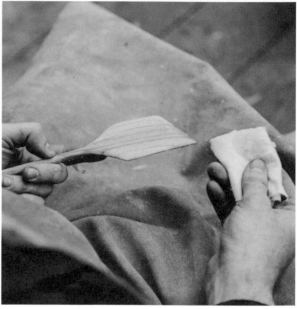

6 Once you are happy with the shape and balance of the spatula you can move on to sanding. It is really important to get a fine, crisp finish on the bevel, giving you a utensil that is easy to use as well as being beautifully formed. To maintain the definition of the bevel, avoid rounding the end off too much when sanding.

7 Give the spatula a rub down to remove any sawdust. Apply a thick coat of beeswax salve and allow it to soak in overnight. Buff any excess off the next morning to give you a clean finish.

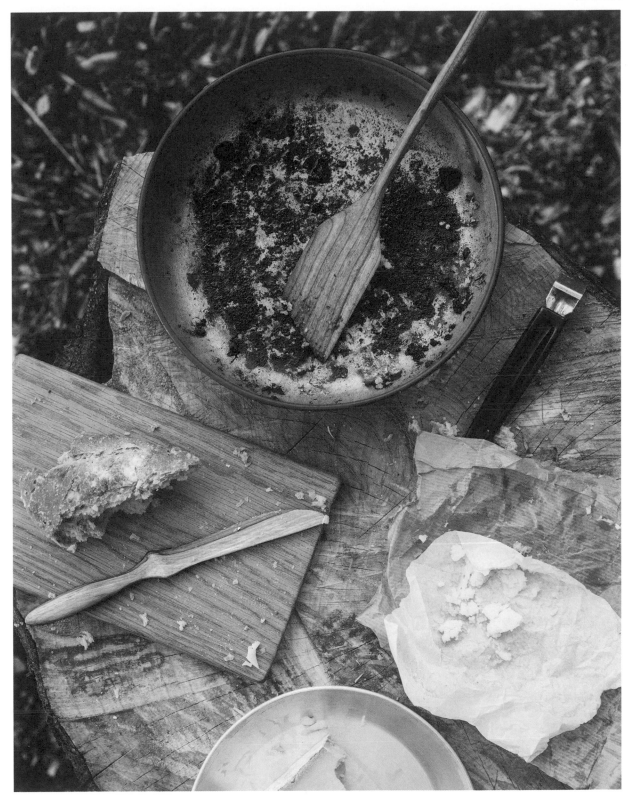

3

COOKING SPOON

Make a cooking spoon using reclaimed walnut

A cooking spoon is something everyone has in their kitchen and uses on a daily basis. When I designed this spoon I wanted to make something that has a delicate aesthetic but is in fact incredibly strong and, most importantly, usable. Carving this cooking spoon will build on the techniques you have used when making the spatula. Similar principles will apply to working the handle and you will be able to practise refining a much larger bowl of a spoon. You may not need to use a jigsaw if the shape of the piece of wood you are starting with is a similar size and shape to your end design, just draw out your template and start carving with a straight knife.

Tools:
pencil
template (paper/card)
jigsaw with curve cut blade
crook knife
straight knife
sandpaper
cloth
beeswax salve

Wood:
walnut

All the walnut I work with comes from a local cabinetmaker. He has plenty of offcuts that are too small for him to use but are perfect for making spoons from. Walnut is a great choice of wood for making cooking spoons from as it is strong, flexible and handles moisture well.

1 Use a template to mark out your shape on your piece of walnut. To minimise waste, angle the handle to one side, which means you should be able to get two spoons from the same piece of wood. When marking out, try to avoid any knots or cracks in the wood as these can weaken the handle or create a hole in the bowl of the spoon.

2 Secure your workpiece to a bench and cut out using a jigsaw with a curve cut blade. Leave around a millimetre of material around the template line. This will allow you to work right up to the perimeter when carving without worrying about cutting through the edge of the bowl.

3 Start to carve out the bowl of the spoon with the crook knife, working from the furthest side of the bowl towards yourself using the scoop cut. You will need to move the spoon around in your supporting hand without altering the cutting grip to ensure you get an even cut distribution.

4 You can also use the push cut with the crook knife, which allows you to shape the rim more accurately and get a regular depth across the bowl of the spoon.

5 Once the bowl of the spoon has reached the depth you are happy with, you can start to shape the handle using the straight knife and the pull cut as you did for the spatula.

6   Now you can start to refine the shape of the back of the bowl and the shoulders with the straight knife, using a combination of both the push cut and detail cut. Keep removing waste material until you are happy with the thickness of the bowl and the join of the shoulders.

7   It is a good idea to take some time with the detail cut to even out the rim of the spoon, making sure you achieve a consistent thickness all the way around. This will make sanding a lot easier as you won't need to remove waste material through sanding.

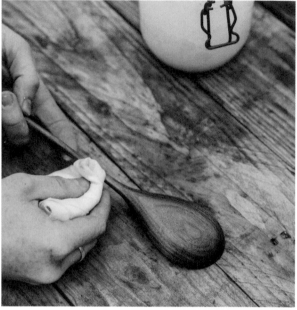

8 Sand the spoon, working with the grain of the wood. You will find the bowl of the spoon needs more sanding to even out the surface. I find manipulating the sandpaper and wrapping a section around your thumb or finger works well, as this allows you more control and gives you a feel for the surface texture as you are sanding.

9 Walnut dust is extremely fine so make sure to give the spoon a thorough rub down with a cloth before applying a good layer of beeswax salve. Allow to soak in overnight, then rub down with a clean cloth the following day.

4

BUTTER KNIFE

Carve a butter knife from cherry

The butter knife is the perfect project for refining your knife work. You will be using one knife in this project, showing you that with the right application you can achieve a varied range of shapes and finishes with a single tool. The butter knife is a tricky utensil to make due to it being small with a detailed shape. However, you will learn to control small detailed cuts and experiment with the shape that feels most comfortable in your own hand. If you have drawn out your shape and there is not a lot of waste material around your design, then you may not need to use the jigsaw, just use the straight knife to remove the waste wood.

Tools:
pencil
template (paper/card)
jigsaw with curve cut blade
straight knife
sandpaper
cloth
beeswax salve

Wood:
cherry

Cherry is a perfect choice of wood for a butter knife as it has a close grain and is very hard when dry so will stand up to daily use very well. Another reason I choose to make butter knives from cherry is to display the amazing colours that run through the heartwood. With the right selection of timber, you can make a utensil that has beautiful figuring, showing off the wood to its best advantage.

1 Make your template. Start by choosing the section you want to make your butter knife from. With cherry, the heartwood has fantastic variations in colour so deciding where to position and draw out your template is key.

2 Secure the workpiece to the workbench and using a jigsaw cut out the butter knife blank, making sure to use a curve cut blade to cut round the narrow shape accurately.

3 Start by working the blade section of the butter knife with the straight knife. Using the scissor cut, start thinning out the shape by keeping the blade of your cutting knife flat to the surface. This will allow you to remove thin slivers of waste material.

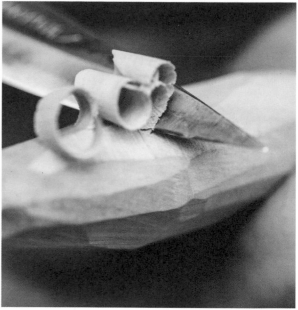

4 Now start working on the join between the blade and the shoulders of the butter knife as it transitions into the handle. Use the push cut to create short curls as you start to define the curves of the shoulders.

5 When you have removed enough waste material you can start refining the shape of the handle using the detail cut. To do this, work slowly from the shoulders down to the end of the handle, concentrating on producing a comfortable shape which sits well in the hand.

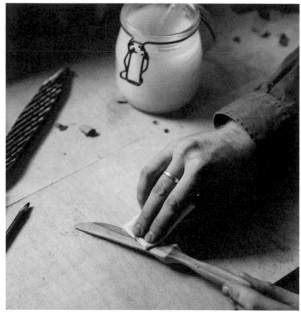

6 Before starting to sand the butter knife, think about the grain direction. As the curves of the handle meet the blade it can be slightly awkward to sand with the grain, but it is important that you try to achieve this to get a clean finish. To do so, move the workpiece around in your hands to find the angle that works best. Work up through the grits of sandpaper starting at 120grit moving through to 320grit.

7 Give the butter knife a wipe down with a cloth to remove any sawdust and apply a generous coat of the beeswax salve. Leave to soak overnight and then buff off with a clean cloth the next morning.

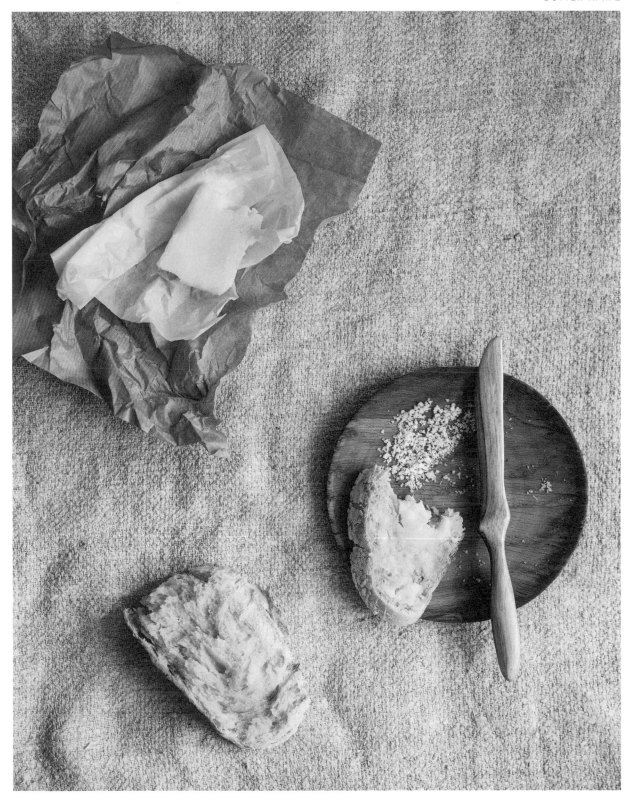

5

COFFEE SCOOP

Use sweet chestnut to carve a coffee scoop

This is possibly one of my favourite designs to make. It uses a lot of different techniques and can be quite challenging as you are working on something that is relatively small. There are many different elements that require strength and concentration to achieve. The techniques you will learn making this scoop will allow you to make any number of other designs and shapes of scoop or spoon with a deep bowl. Although I use and make these scoops for coffee, they can equally be used for any other dry goods.

Tools:
pencil
template (paper/card)
jigsaw with curve cut blade
crook knife
straight knife
sandpaper
cloth
beeswax salve

Wood:
sweet chestnut

Sweet chestnut is sometimes referred to as 'poor man's oak' but I think it is probably one of my favourite of the native hardwoods we have in the UK. It is incredibly versatile and its colour can vary hugely, giving you tones of lightest tan right through to a deep chocolate brown. Its grain can run true and straight and then surprise you with fantastic swirls and patterns, which is something to take into consideration when working with it, as these can make it trickier to carve with.

1 Selecting the right piece of timber is especially important for this project. Choose a section where the grain is running nice and straight and make sure you check the timber all the way around for any signs of knots or cracks. The bowl on the coffee scoop is quite deep and you need to make sure there are no defects running through it. Once you have selected a section, mark out your design using a template, taking time to ensure the bowl of the spoon is spherical.

2 Using a jigsaw with a curve cut blade, cut out the shape, taking extra care as your piece of wood will be thicker than previous projects in this book due to the depth of the bowl of the scoop. You may need to work quite slowly to ensure a clean cut.

3 Once you have your blank cut out, start working on the bowl of the scoop with the crook knife. The scoop cut will work well to remove a good deal of waste material, and then the push cut can be used to refine the shape and make the bowl deeper.

4 Moving on to shaping the scoop, use the straight knife to start to remove stock material from the back of the bowl. You will be able to take off large amounts at once using the scissor cut. Remember to change the direction you are cutting by reversing the direction of the scoop in your hands. This will ensure you avoid cutting against the grain.

5 Take some time using the detail cut to create nice fluid transitions from the shoulders down to the end of the handle. Once you are happy with the shape of your handle, using the straight knife, revisit the bowl of the scoop to achieve an even thickness on the rim. You can shave small amounts off the top by keeping the blade very flat to the surface of the wood as you did when carving the cooking spoon.

6 When you are happy with the shape, you can begin sanding. Move through the grits (from 120 to 320grit) until it is smooth to the touch and there are no obvious scratches from the coarser sandpaper.

7 Give the scoop a wipe down and a good coating of the beeswax salve. Allow this to soak in overnight and then rub away any excess left on the surface the following morning.

CHOPPING BOARD

Make a functional chopping board from reclaimed maple

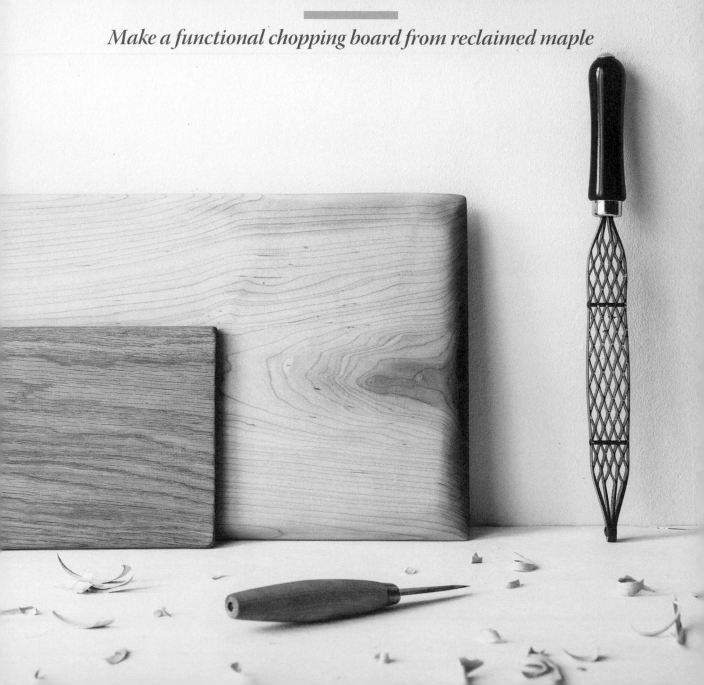

A chopping board is an essential in anyone's kitchen. This is a really simple and functional design that will introduce you to using the Japanese saw rasp and start you working on something that is larger in scale than a utensil. The board shown is a relatively large one, but you can make yours any size you want depending on the size of wood you are able to get hold of.

Tools:
pencil
straight knife
clamp
Japanese saw rasp
sandpaper
cloth
beeswax salve

Wood:
maple

I am using a slab of maple that I sourced from the offcuts pile at a local timber merchant. Maple is a great wood to use for a chopping board as it is so close grained. This means it is far easier to keep clean as there is little to no chance of food getting trapped in any open or raised wood grain. Its density and strength also means it will stand up to being regularly used to chop food. Other good alternative hardwoods I would recommend are sycamore, beech and walnut.

1 The piece of maple I am using is an offcut from what would have been a large plank of timber. I am going to be using pretty much the whole piece and just rounding off the edges. You don't need to make a template for this, just mark a line in from the edge of the board as a guide for where you want the bevel to begin.

2 With the straight knife and using the pull cut, start to remove stock from the longest sides of the board. Make sure you switch between the two sides of the board to keep the bevel even.

3 Now start working the shorter ends of the chopping board using a combination of the pull cut and the push cut. As you are cutting across the grain the use of the two different cuts is important in order to get a smooth and even finish.

4 Once you have removed a good deal of waste material and you are happy with the shape of the bevel, you can concentrate on shaping the corners. I have chosen to bring the corners to a point using the push cut, however you could round them off depending on your own design.

5 Now clamp the board to a workbench and start to use the saw rasp. The saw rasp cuts on the push stroke, so you can only use it in one direction, not back and forth like a conventional saw. It also has a coarse and a fine side. Start by shaping the edges using the coarse side and then when you are happy with the shape you can use the fine side of the rasp to blend in any faceted edges.

6 The fine side of the rasp will give you a finish similar to using coarse sandpaper. When you start sanding, it is important to move up through the grits of sandpaper so that you are creating an even finish. Finishing on a 320grit will give you a smooth silky surface. It is worth taking some time with the rasp and sandpaper to achieve a quality finish.

7 Once the board has been sanded and wiped down, apply a very generous coating of beeswax salve and let it soak in overnight with the board propped on its end. Rub down and polish the surface the following day.

7

SERVING BOARD

Use reclaimed oak to carve a serving board

Making a serving board is a good way to use the skills learnt from spoon carving on a project that requires the use of new tools and techniques. I show you how to utilise the shape of reclaimed timber to inform a design rather than trying to find the perfect piece of wood to fit a pre-determined shape. And, more often than not, you end up with a more interesting board this way. It is a really nice way to work as it allows for shapes and curves to develop naturally and gives you the opportunity to allow the grain and texture of the wood to take centre stage.

Tools:
pencil
template (paper/card)
jigsaw with curve cut blade
clamp
straight knife
drill
sandpaper
cloth
beeswax salve

Wood:
oak

You can often come across reclaimed oak in the form of old floorboards and discarded shelves. It tends to already be the perfect width and thickness to make serving boards from. The oak I use in this project is an offcut from a local cabinetmaker. Being able to source reclaimed lengths of timber in this form is ideal as no professional power tools or equipment are required. A jigsaw should be all that you need.

1 Mark out the shape of the serving board on the piece of wood with a pencil. Either use a template or draw freehand, depending on the design you have in mind.

2 Cut out your design using a jigsaw, taking care around the tight corners. Clamp your piece of wood to a workbench or stable surface to ensure you make the cut safely. You will need to use a curve cut blade in your jigsaw in order to make a clean cut following your design.

3 Start by shaping the handle with the straight knife using the pull cut. Once you have rounded off the length of the handle you can use a push cut to shape the curve at the top. This is a good example of where you will encounter a change of direction in the grain. The best way to combat this is to keep pivoting your board so you are cutting from opposing directions.

4 Next, drill the hole in the handle. The size of the hole you want will depend on how big you decide to make your board. Choose the right sized drill bit to ensure the hole is the correct size.

5 Once you have the hole drilled you can use the very tip of your straight knife to tidy up and shape the edges.

6 After you have shaped the handle of the board, you can start to look at the shoulders. Here, a combination of the detail cut and push cut is useful to get a graceful sweep and to ensure that the transition from the handle to shoulders is smooth.

7 You can soften and round off the sides of the board by working along each side following the grain. By using a pull cut again you are aiming to refine the shape by removing nice thin, even, ribbon-like shavings, keeping your blade flat to the workpiece.

8 Once you have shaped the board and are happy with the finish you have achieved with the straight knife, you can move on to sanding to even out the surface and give a lovely finish. Always working with the grain of the wood, start to sand and refine the edges moving up through the grits until you get to 320grit.

9 Give the board a thorough wipe down with a cloth to make sure you have removed as much sawdust as possible. Using a clean rag to apply a coat of the beeswax salve, leave it to soak overnight and wipe off any excess the following morning.

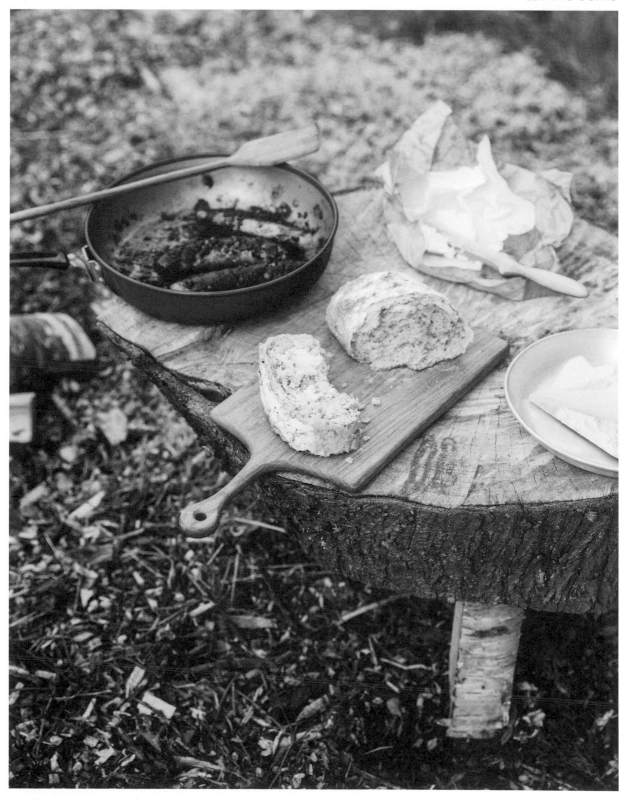

8

SMALL OAK BOWL

Using green oak to carve a small oak bowl

This project is a great introduction to making vessels. I am a wood turner as well as a wood carver, so making bowls, pots and vessels is something I'm really passionate about. Carving a bowl is, in principle, the same as turning one but the results are very different. Maybe it is the time that goes into it or the fact that you can see the effect every cut makes. Carving a bowl in this project will teach you how to use carving gouges, which are a great addition to your tool set.

Tools:
compass
pencil
clamp
10mm carving gouge
6mm carving gouge
jigsaw
straight knife
crook knife
sandpaper
cloth
beeswax salve

Wood:
green oak

Oak is a fantastically versatile material. When it is green it is easily workable with hand tools, and when it dries it is immensely strong. I explain how to process green wood, but you can easily use dry offcuts or reclaimed timber in its place. The reason I suggest using green wood is to make it easier when using the carving gouges, so if you can get hold of a freshly cut branch you will find the work easier going.

1 Start by using a compass to mark out the diameter of your bowl. The size of your bowl will be determined by the size of your piece of wood. I am using a slab of green oak that I cut up from a log using a chainsaw, but splitting a smaller branch in two with an axe will work just as well.

2 Clamp the wood in place on a stable work surface and using the 10mm gouge, start to work across the grain from the near side of the bowl away from you. Make sure never to work towards yourself when using carving gouges. You may find it easier to stand up for this stage as it will allow you to put some weight behind your cut whilst keeping maximum control over the tool. Rather than trying to take as much waste away at once, focus on removing even curls with your gouge. This will be less tiring in the long run.

3 When you have reached the depth you are happy with you can begin to use the 6mm gouge to neaten up the edges and work right up to the perimeter line. You will need to start rotating the workpiece and to switch between the 10mm gouge to remove the bulk of the waste and the 6mm gouge to refine the inside of the bowl.

4 Once you have a smooth even inside surface, you can use the jigsaw to cut the bowl out. Make sure that the blade of the jigsaw is long enough to cut through the thickness of the wood. You may need to go slowly to ensure a smooth cut.

5 Now start to carve the outside of the bowl with the straight knife. You need to use a variation of the pull cut using your thumb as an anchor point and cutting towards yourself with a clenching action. This cut will feel similar to the scoop cut when using your crook knife. Again take great care and remain aware of exactly where your fingers are, as you will be working in close proximity to the blade.

6 Once you have shaped the outside you can use the crook knife to even out the inside surface of the bowl and remove the chisel marks. The scoop cut and the push cut will work well here, but remember exactly where your fingers are positioned in relation to the knife to avoid possible injury. Sitting down and working close to your body will also help with stability and control.

7 Once you are happy with the depth of the bowl and the wall thickness (you can use a detail cut on the underside of the bowl to ensure that it is sitting flat on the bottom), take a moment to refine the rim of the bowl. Use the top of the straight knife blade to remove very small amounts of material. Leave the bowl to dry out for a few days before finishing. To aid the drying process you can wrap it in newspaper, but do not leave it near a direct heat source as this may cause it to split.

8 Once the bowl has dried out it will feel considerably lighter as the moisture content should have dropped. You can begin to sand the bowl, starting with the inside working with 120grit sandpaper to even out the surface and remove any bumps quite quickly, then moving through the grits to achieve a smooth finish. The outside of the bowl can be sanded in exactly the same way.

9 Give the bowl a good wipe down with a cloth and apply a generous amount of the beeswax salve. Let it sink in overnight before buffing off the following morning.

FACETING A COFFEE SCOOP

Although I finish most of my projects with sandpaper, sometimes I like to create a finish that just uses the knife blade. By making small, clean cuts that give a texture to the surface of the wood, you can create lots of individual planes that reflect the light and give a fantastic textured finish. You have to have a very sharp knife to do this, so it is a good idea to hone your blade before starting the finishing cuts. For further detail, see page 124 before embarking on this project.

Tools:
pencil
straight knife
sandpaper
cloth
beeswax salve

1 This project shows how to facet the back of a coffee scoop. This technique is really effective on this shape of spoon, as there is a large surface area to work on. Start with a scoop that is already fashioned to its finished state apart from the back of the bowl (see the coffee scoop on page 76). Draw a horizontal line across the back of the bowl.

2 Start by making small controlled cuts using the detail cut. Work firstly from the middle point up to the top of the scoop. Do this very gradually, so you start to see what length and size of facet you like the look of.

3 Now begin working the other way, from the middle down towards the handle. This will ensure you get nice clean cuts without picking up the grain. Using the detail cut to take off small chips of wood, try to keep the depth and size of cut as consistent as possible. Remember this is going to be the surface finish, so you are aiming to keep the overall shape while still adding texture.

4 Once all the cuts have been made, take some time to check over the surface to make sure you are happy with the finish. It's also worth thinking about where the facet cuts stop in relation to the handle. You can have a clear line where the texture starts or you can use sandpaper to make a smooth transition.

5 When you are happy with the finish, give the workpiece a wipe with a cloth to remove any sawdust and apply a coat of the beeswax salve. This will give the facets a real shine and reflect the light even more.

Scorching

SCORCHING A COOKING SPOON

Scorching is a really effective and simple way to change the appearance and colour of wood without losing the grain. It is a technique that works on many different types of wood, although I have found hardwoods to be the most effective. In this project the handle of the walnut cooking spoon (see page 60) is scorched, which leaves it with a beautifully glossy, dark shine. Scorching only part of the spoon accentuates the graceful sweep of the shoulders as the handle transitions into the head. Although this is just one example of how to use this technique, I encourage you to experiment in applying it to other objects, be they spoons or boards, to create different finishes. You will need to make sure that you have a surface to work on that you do not mind getting a bit charred. A bit of old scaffolding board or plywood works well. It is also advisable to work in a well-ventilated area as you produce smoke when working with the blowtorch.

Tools:
blowtorch
protective gloves
protective goggles
cloths
sandpaper
beeswax salve

For this project you need a spoon where the head has been sanded to its final finish but the handle has only been roughly sanded and shaped using 120grit sandpaper. This is because when you scorch the surface of the wood, the surface layer will burn and create a fine, almost charcoal-like layer. This is then sanded with a fine grit sandpaper to remove any excess.

——

'Scorching only part of the spoon accentuates the graceful sweep of the shoulders as the handle transitions into the head'

——

1 Hold the blowtorch in your dominant hand, and keep the end of the torch about 5cm from the spoon. Work up and down the length of the handle, rotating the spoon with your free hand as you go to ensure an even distribution of charring.

2 Once you have scorched all of the desired area on the spoon and it has cooled down, give it a wipe down with a cloth and start to sand, working your way up through the different grits.

3 As you sand, wipe down the handle between each change of grit. You may need to re-scorch areas after sanding and keep repeating the process until you have complete coverage.

4 Keep rubbing down the handle until nothing comes off onto the cloth. You can now apply a coat of the beeswax salve. It is best to use a different cloth to apply salve to the head of the spoon to prevent any of the scorched sawdust from the handle staining the un-scorched wood.

Ebonising

EBONISING A
SMALL OAK BOWL

The ebonising process is one that is hard to believe even when you see it happening before your eyes. The basic principle is to create a chemical reaction between the natural tannins found in wood and iron oxide. Tannin is a tree's natural defence against predators and iron oxide is what we commonly know as rust. You can create an iron solution by steeping wire wool or iron nails in vinegar. Then by applying this to the surface of a wood that is high in tannin, such as oak, you can produce a chemical reaction that turns the wood black. Depending on the levels of tannin found in the wood, you will achieve different depths of black from blue and purple hues to rich, jet blacks. In this project I show you how to ebonise a small oak bowl (see page 98). I advise using either oak or walnut for ebonising due to the high tannin content in both woods.

Tools:
jar or container
water
white distilled vinegar
iron nails or wire wool
paintbrush
cloths

'The ebonising process is one that is hard to believe even when you see it happening before your eyes'

1 Fill a large jar or container with two parts water to one part white vinegar and add the nails or wire wool and leave. Within a week the liquid should start to turn an orange brown colour as the iron starts to go rusty. Do not keep a lid on your jar as a small amount of gas will be produced as the vinegar reacts with the iron, which will need to escape.

2 Once the nails have been in the solution for at least a week, a layer of rust will form on the surface and the liquid will be brown or orange in colour.

3 Using a paintbrush, start applying the rusty vinegar solution to the surface of the wood and allow the reaction to take place. If you are using oak, the reaction will happen straight away and you can see the colour change in front of you. Observe how the colour is developing and keep applying more solution if you wish to intensify it.

4 You can keep applying layers, allowing each layer time to dry, until the colour does not get any darker. Once you are happy with the colour, you can give the surface of the wood a wipe down with a cloth. This may result in some of the colour rubbing off, but keep going until nothing more comes off on the cloth. You may want to leave the ebonised object somewhere to dry to allow the vinegar odour to evaporate.

5 When it is completely dry, apply a coat of the beeswax salve. You will need to use a clean cloth just in case any residual pigment comes off the object as you apply the salve. Leave to sink in overnight and then rub down the following day.

SANDING

Sanding is a process that not every wood carver chooses to do. It is down to personal preference and I have found that I prefer the finish and appearance that it gives. Every project in the book can be made with the sanding process left out. However, for me sanding gives the finished object that extra bit of refinement and produces something that has simplicity and elegance in its form. It also has practical applications. Sanding the bowl of an eating or cooking spoon produces a smooth surface that reduces the chance of food getting trapped and makes it easier to clean.

I use four different grades of sandpaper, 120grit being the coarsest, moving up through 180grit, 240grit to 320grit, which is the finest. Working up through the different grits is really important, when you start with a coarse paper such as a 120grit, it creates quite prominent scratch marks that you can see with the naked eye. As you then move up through the grits the scratch patterns become finer and finer, until you cannot see the scratch patterns on the surface without magnification.

One of the most important things to remember when sanding is always to sand with (in the direction of) the grain of the wood and never across it. If you sand across the grain you will find it very difficult to smooth the scratches out

'For me sanding gives the finished object that extra bit of refinement and produces something that has simplicity and elegance in its form'

later. Sanding with the grain allows the grit on the paper to smooth the surface of the wood without any tearing of the fibres on the surface. When you use sandpaper, the surface of the paper will start to clog with a fine layer of wood dust. If you find this happens, wipe the sandpaper on a surface that the fine dust will cling on to, such as a leather or denim apron. You will find that sanding by hand does take time, but the finish you get will be well worth the time and effort you have put in.

Beeswax salve

There are many different products on the market that you can use as a finish on wood but I make and use my own beeswax salve to treat every piece of woodenware that I carve. It is a simple recipe that produces a gentle finish, which can be applied to the surface of wood to bring out the natural colour and patina of the grain. As well as giving the product a protective coating against moisture, it is completely food-safe: everything treated with it is usable and washable.

This recipe will give you a large Kilner jar of salve, which should last you a good amount of time.

Tools and materials:
1 litre pure mineral oil
500g pure beeswax pellets
large saucepan
heat source
Kilner jar
tea towel

1 The basic ratio is two parts mineral oil to one part beeswax. Start by measuring out 500g of beeswax pellets and 1 litre of mineral oil. Sterilise the Kilner jar using boiling water, or put it through a dishwasher cycle.

2 Pour the oil into a large saucepan and set the heat to its lowest setting. Add the beeswax and heat gently until the pellets start to dissolve. Stir very gently to ensure the two ingredients have combined thoroughly. As soon as the mixture is clear, remove from the heat and set aside to cool.

3 Allow the beeswax and oil to cool for 5–10 minutes and then pour the mixture into the Kilner jar. Take care in case the liquid is still hot.

4 Set aside and leave the lid open. Place a tea towel over the jar to ensure nothing drops in. Allow the salve to cure overnight and once it is completely cool it will set and turn cloudy. It is then ready to use.

5 Put a rubber seal on the jar and store in a cool, dark place.

TOOL CARE

Keeping your tools sharp and making sure they are well maintained is a really important part of a craftsman's practice. Dull or blunt tools can be dangerous and it is always far safer to have a sharp blade to work with than a blunt one. A sharp blade is far more predictable and allows you greater control than a dull one. The less pressure and force you have to apply on the knife to make the cut the better.

I am going to explain how to sharpen both your straight knife and crook knife, and with a little practice you will soon notice the difference. Sharpening is something that can take a little while before you

'Dull or blunt tools can be dangerous'

become proficient, but once you have cracked it, you will be able to put a razor sharp finish on your tools every single time.

I learned very quickly to appreciate the value of having sharp tools. Carving becomes effortless and the control and detail in your work is far more sophisticated as a result. A good indicator of having successfully sharpened your blades is the sound a cut makes through wood. I liken it to the sound of fresh snow crunching underfoot. I have tried quite a few different ways of sharpening, from grinding wheels to sharpening systems, but I have come to the conclusion that sometimes the simplest really is the best.

Here I will show you how to create some basic tools to sharpen both your knives.

Straight knife

Tools and materials:
waterproof container
water
water-stone
Autosol (or alternative brand of metal polish)
leather strop (real leather)
cotton cloth

1 Fill your container with water and submerge the water-stone. Leave it to soak for 10–15 minutes and you will begin to see air bubbles escaping.

2 Once the water-stone has stopped releasing air bubbles, place it on a flat surface making sure the surface of the stone is still wet. You can splash a little on from the container if necessary. Make sure the coarse side of the stone is facing up, as this will be used first.

3 Place the bevel of the blade flat on the surface of the stone, holding the handle in one hand. Applying pressure on the blade with the other hand, keep the blade flat to the stone and push the blade away from you up the length of the stone.

4 Starting at the opposite end on the stone, place the other side of the knife bevel flat on the stone. Supporting it in the same way, pull the blade towards yourself down the length of the stone. If you are just refreshing the surface, you only need to make 10–15 passes on each side of the blade. Make sure you keep the surface of the stone wet throughout. If you have pitted your blade, repeat this motion until you have a clean edge.

5 Now turn the stone over to the fine side and wet the surface to repeat the process. This is more of a honing process than a sharpening. Working on this side of the stone will polish the edge and remove the burr created when sharpening.

6 Finally apply a small amount of the Autosol metal polish to the surface of the leather strop, or belt, and rub it in. Place the bevel of the blade flat on the surface at the bottom of the strop and pull the blade up towards yourself. Do this 10 times on each side of the blade.

7 When the surface has a shiny, polished finish, give the blade a wipe with a cloth. Take care, the edge will now be razor sharp.

Crook knife

Tools and materials:
wet and dry sandpaper (600grit and 1500grit)
2 x strips of soft leather
3 x lengths of wood (30cm long x 4.5cm wide x
  1cm deep)
PVA glue
3 x lengths of dowel (22cm long x 2cm diameter)
marker pen
Autosol (or alternative metal polish)
cotton cloth

1 Start by cutting one 25cm x 12cm strip of the 600grit wet and dry sandpaper, one 25cm x 12cm strip of the 1500grit wet and dry, and one 25cm x 12cm strip of the soft leather. Now glue each of these strips to one of the lengths of wood, wrapping each strip right around the wood, making sure the join finishes down the middle of one side. With the leather, make sure you have good contact and adhesion between the surface of the wood and the underside of the leather.

2 Repeat this first stage and cut three further strips now measuring 12cm x 10cm and glue each one round a length of dowel. These round sharpening tools you have made will allow you to get inside the curve of the crook knife.

3 Using the marker pen, colour in the bevel of the blade. This will enable you to see where you have made contact with the sandpaper. If there is ink left on the blade you will know you have not made contact on that particular part.

4 Begin by sharpening the outside curve of the blade with the flat sharpening tools. Do each side of the blade separately. Start with the 600grit and pull the flat tool across the bevel working from the top down towards the edge of the blade. Only work in this direction, never back and forth or you will dull the blade. Once you have removed all the ink from the bevel with the 600grit paper, re-ink the bevel and repeat the process using the 1500grit. You will notice the difference in the surface finish as it starts to become a lot shinier. Once you completed this process of one side of the blade, switch and repeat on the other.

5 Now move on to the inside curve. Using the rounded 600grit sanding bar, make a few strokes on the inside curve of the blade, keeping the surface of the paper as flat to the blade as possible. Move on to the 1500grit sanding bar and repeat the process on both sides of the blade.

6 Now add a little of the Autosol metal polish to the surface of the flat leather strop and start to work across the outside bevel using the same motion as you did when sharpening. This will remove the fine burr that builds up during sharpening.

7 Repeat the same process with the leather strop on the dowel for the inside curve of the blade.

8 When the surface has a shiny, polished finish, give the blade a wipe with a cloth, taking care as the edge will now be razor sharp.

TOOL ROLL

Having spent all that time and effort sharpening your tools it is important to store them safely to ensure they remain in good condition. Keeping them protected means they will hold their edges for longer and require less sharpening over time. A tool roll is a really easy way of doing this and here I show you how to make a really simple one, which will give you somewhere to store your knives. I used a heavyweight canvas and a scrap of thick brown cotton but any material you have to hand will work. The heavier the weight of fabric the better, as this will give you more protection when folding over the fabric lip to cover the blades. I used a sewing machine to assemble the tool roll but if you do not have access to one, hand stitching will work just as well. The only difference will be the time it takes to put it together.

Tools and materials:
heavyweight fabric (canvas, cotton, wool, denim or
   leather all work well)
ruler
graphite pencil or chalk
sharp scissors
sewing machine
thread
pins
cotton tape

'Keeping tools protected means they will hold their edges for longer and require less sharpening over time'

1 Once you have all your materials laid out, mark out one rectangle measuring 38cm x 56cm on the canvas and another rectangle measuring 34cm x 15cm on the thick brown cotton. Take a sharp pair of scissors and accurately cut along the lines until you have your two pieces of fabric to work with.

2 Fold the larger rectangle of canvas in half lengthways and sew up the two opposite shorter sides. A simple running stitch on the sewing machine will work fine.

3 Turn the canvas inside out so that the raw seams are no longer visible. You can use the end of a pencil to push the corners gently out giving you crisp, defined points.

4 Place the smaller rectangle of brown fabric in line with the bottom, open edge of canvas. Make sure it is centred and equidistant from both sides. Pin along the bottom roughly 4cm in from the edge. Sew through all three layers with a running stitch, attaching the brown fabric and sewing up the open edge of the canvas.

5 Now you can sew the two short sides of the brown fabric in position so it is completely attached to the canvas back.

6 Using your chalk or graphite pencil, divide the brown rectangle into six equal pockets and mark them with lines. Sew along each line,

'Once they are in, you can fold over the top of the canvas to protect the blades and roll'

making sure to reverse stitch at the beginning and end of every line to secure the thread.

7 Cut two pieces of cotton tape 40cm long and lay them out on the back of the tool roll, facing opposite directions. Pin these in place ready to attach.

8 Sew two parallel lines through each piece of tape to secure it in place. Make sure to remove the pins as you sew to avoid breaking your needle.

9 Your tool roll is now ready. Put your knives in the pockets and test that they fit. Once they are in, you can fold over the top of the canvas to protect the blades and roll up. Wrap the ties around and fasten in a knot.

RESOURCES

All of the tools and materials used throughout this book can be found in local DIY stores and online, but here I list a few of my favourite suppliers for you to look at. My wish was to write a book that allowed people to get into carving without having to invest in expensive tools and set-up. It is always worth doing your research to see what is available locally to you. No matter where you are in the world you will be able to access everything you need to start carving. I work full-time at my business Forest + Found and happily respond to those individuals who contact me for advice. I have included my contact details below in case you would like to do the same.

WOODLAND CRAFT SUPPLIES
www.woodlandcraftsupplies.co.uk
email: matthew_robinson_uk@yahoo.com
Items I source from this supplier:
Mora 120 straight knife
Mora 162 crook knife
Gransfors Wildlife Hatchet
Japanese Combination Water-stone

AXMINSTER TOOLS & MACHINERY
www.axminster.co.uk
email: cs@axminster.co.uk
Items I source from this supplier:
Japanese saw rasp (Shinto)
carving gouges (Kirschen)
Wet & Dry Sandpaper (Silicon carbide) 600grit – 1500grit

ITS
www.its.co.uk
email: sales@its.co.uk
Items I source from this supplier:
drill
jigsaw
curve cut blade

WOOD FINISHES DIRECT
www.wood-finishes-direct.com
Items I source from this supplier:
sandpaper 120grit – 320grit

AMAZON
www.amazon.co.uk
Items I source from this supplier:
mineral oil
pure beeswax
Autosol metal polish

FOREST + FOUND
www.forest-and-found.com
email: contact@forest-and-found.com

GLOSSARY

Autosol: a common brand of metal polish.

axe: a tool used for working greenwood.

bevel: the sloping surface or edge of a blade or cutting edge.

blank: the rough shape of a spoon cut out of wood prior to carving.

bowl: the concave head of a spoon.

bulk waste: excess wood that needs to be removed before defining the shape of an object.

burr: the rough edge left on a blade after sharpening.

carving gouge: a chisel with a concave blade.

close-grained: when the fibres of wood are packed tightly together to form dense wood.

concave: a surface that curves inwards.

curve cut blade: a specific jigsaw blade for cutting curves.

crook knife: a wood carving knife with a curved blade for hollowing.

ebonising: the process of using the chemical reaction between tannin and iron oxide to turn wood black.

faceting: a surface finish produced with the blade of a knife.

figuring: the distinctive patterning in wood grain.

finishing cut: the final cuts made with a knife before sanding.

Forestry Commission: the government department in charge of woodlands in England and Scotland.

grain direction: the direction in which the fibres are running through a piece of wood.

greenwood: freshly cut wood with a high moisture content.

grit: the grade of sandpaper from coarse (120grit) to fine (320grit).

hardwood: dense wood suitable for carving, from broad-leaved trees.

heartwood: the dense inner part of a tree trunk, which produces the hardest timber.

honing: the final stages of sharpening a blade, this removes any burr.

iron oxide: the chemical compound made up of iron and oxygen, which naturally occurs as rust.

knot: a tight whorl in the grain where a branch would have formed.

Local Authority: an administrative body such as a local council.

pure beeswax: beeswax without the addition of paraffin, used in most commercial polishing products, making it food-safe.

running stitch: a straight stitch, the most common used on a sewing machine.

saw rasp: a tool made up of double-edged saw blades.

scorching: the process of burning to create a blackened effect on wood.

shoulders: the transition between a handle and body of a utensil or board.

stock material: excess wood which has to be removed before defining the shape of an object.

storm-damaged: a tree that has been blown over or hit by lightning.

straight knife: a wood carving knife with a straight blade.

tannin: an organic acid present in trees as a natural defence system.

tree surgeon: A person who prunes or treats old or damaged trees.

water-stone: a sharpening stone that uses water as a lubricant.

wet and dry: a high grade of very fine sandpaper.

wood grain: the fibres running through the wood that form its pattern.

workpiece: The object being carved or worked on during a project.

INDEX

LAST WORDS

Carving is a craft that has been practiced for hundreds of years, creating both functional and beautiful objects throughout history, it is my hope that we keep this heritage craft alive and keep on making for hundreds of years to come.

I hope this book and the projects within it have given you the confidence and knowledge to go forward and work on your own designs, shapes and forms.

Writing this book has been journey. I have met some amazing and talented people along the way and without them it would not have been possible.

I think I should start by thanking Judith from Kyle Books. When she first got in contact, asking if I would be interested in writing this book, my first reaction was, 'What, me?'. And I'm so glad she did as it has been a truly wonderful experience and has given me the confidence in my own work that I perhaps lacked, so I want to say thank you to her for having the confidence in my work to see the potential of it translating into book form.

I want to say a big thank you to Kyle of Kyle Books, she allowed this project to go ahead and without her support and backing this would not have been possible. Sophie Allen, my editor, has been a massive part of the whole process; she has managed to decode my overly excited rambling emails, reigned in perhaps slightly over-ambitious and sometimes dangerous ideas and has generally made the day-to-day of writing and constructing this book joyful.

There would, of course, be no book without the constant hard work and effort from Tina Smith, our amazing designer. From our very first conversation, I knew we were in safe hands and she also has had to put up with my non-sensical ramblings on the phone and has managed to pull out the odd few words that did make sense and transform them into something that is beautifully clean and simple – thank you.

I had clear ideas in my mind of how I wanted the book to look and feel and this is where Dean and Jeska Hearne come in. They have made the book what it is. The constant effort, on their part, from the very first phonecall about working on this project, is humbling. Their vision for every single photograph has resulted in a truly beautiful book. They are two of the nicest, funniest human beings I have ever met and I hope they will remain life-long friends.

I want to say thank you to Troo, Chris, Emma and Adam from Tree Couture. Without their generosity and willingness to help I would not have been able to work with all the beautiful walnut and oak I have used for some of the projects in this book. It's fantastic to be able to work with such amazing craftsmen and I hope to be able to do so for a long time to come.

My family have been the constant throughout this process. My brother, James, and Abi, for popping their heads around the workshop door checking in on me; my mum, Liz or Lis, as she is more affectionately known, offering words of wisdom and advice, not to mention love and support; to my Nana Jean Gray, who passed away in 2013, but one of the last things she said to me that has been a constant source of inspiration was, 'Now you have built the workshop Maxy, you can do anything', and so I am writing this book for her, of which I hope she would be proud.

This brings me to the last person I would like to thank, although there are not really the words to express my love and gratitude towards her – everything I do, everything I write and everything I make would not be possible without the constant love, support and a good measure of tolerance from my beautiful partner Abigail, whom I love.

Thank you.